I AM A JESSE WHITE TUMBLER

*Text and photographs
by Diane Schmidt*

Albert Whitman & Company, Niles, Illinois

Library of Congress Cataloging-in-Publication Data

Schmidt, Diane.
    I am a Jesse White tumbler / Diane Schmidt.
        p.   cm.
      Summary: Kenyon Conner, a member of the inner-city
Jesse White Tumbling Team, describes the team's shows, routines,
and positive aspects and influences.
      ISBN 0-8075-3444-7 (lib. bdg.)
      1. Conner, Kenyon—Juvenile literature.   2. Acrobats—United
States—Biography—Juvenile literature.   3. Jesse White Tumbling Team
—Juvenile literature.   [1. Jesse White Tumbling Team.
2. Tumbling.   3. Conner, Kenyon.]   I. Title.
GV550.2.C66S36   1990   89-16590
796.47'092—dc20   CIP
[B]   AC

Design by Karen Yops

For my father, Dr. John L. Schmidt

Special thanks to Kenyon, who is a shining star and a friend
who has taught me much, and to Jesse White and ALL the Jesse
White Tumblers, who are wonderful and inspiring.
And very special thanks to Kathy Tucker, who saw this project
through from beginning to end; to my mother, Miriam Schmidt,
who asked me to do children's books; and to Lionel Corbett,
my "resounding board."

I'm Kenyon Conner, and I'm a Jesse White Tumbler. The Jesse White Tumbling Team is mostly made up of kids from the Cabrini-Green housing project in Chicago. We do tumbling shows all over the city and across the country.

I got on the team when I was five years old. I knew one of the tumblers, and he told Jesse White, "There's a kid who's a pretty good tumbler," so Mr. White tried me out. He said I could be on the team, so I must have been pretty good.

This is Mr. White and me.

For a while I stopped coming out with the team because of family problems. When I was six, I went to live with my grandmother. I guess my mother didn't want me to stay with her.

Here I am with my grandmother. I call her Momma.

This is me and my dog Red.

Here's some of the family—my grandmother with my cousin Kenneth, me with my little cousin, David, and my cousin Shante with another cousin, Jonita, on her lap. I don't know how many cousins I have—too many! I live with my grandmother, my auntie, three uncles, Kenneth and Shante, and my dogs, Red and Adidas. In this picture I look like my mother.

We used to live at Cabrini-Green. That's where I was born. Cabrini-Green is a group of very big apartment buildings built for people who don't have jobs or much money. About thirteen thousand people live there—it's like a small city. It was fun at Cabrini-Green because I met so many people, but we only had two rooms, so our house is better.

If I wasn't a Jesse White Tumbler, I wouldn't have much to do. I might even belong to a gang. Being on the team helps keep you out of trouble. You can't drink, smoke, swear, take drugs, or have anything to do with gangs. The gangs don't mess with the Jesse White Tumblers, either.

In order to stay on the team, you have to keep up your schoolwork. If you don't, Mr. White will put you off the team until you bring up your grades. I'm in the eighth grade at Lowell School, and so far I'm doing okay. My best subjects are English and math—I'm taking basic algebra this year. I really like school—I like it even better than tumbling.

If a kid is ready and wants to get on the team, I tell him to call Mr. White at his office and arrange to try out. Mr. White will see what the kid can do and tell him when to come back or send him to a training site. There are eleven training sites where team coaches teach tumbling. This year there are 550 kids in the instruction program, and 3,600 more waiting to get in.

You really have to be pretty good to be considered for the Jesse White Tumblers. There are 75 kids on the team. At first there were only boys, but now there are some girls, too.

I used to teach tumbling at the Logan Square Boys' Club. I want to teach again sometime. I like the way it makes me feel. I know I'm a good tumbler when I can help other kids learn.

These kids would like to try out for the team.

That's Tran, Anthony, me, Shawn, and Sam talking before a show. All my friends are tumblers, and we all help each other. My teammates helped me learn tumbling, and I help new kids. Mr. White focuses on the fine points—how to straighten your arms and feet, the right way to hold your head. And he choreographs the routines.

We always use mats, and we "spot" or watch each other carefully in practice until we've mastered a stunt. Sometimes someone is there to catch you if you fall, but not always. A couple of years ago I overrotated on a forward flip, landed on my arm, and broke it. It hurt a lot. The worst thing that could happen is you could injure your neck and become paralyzed. Mr. White always tells the audience not to try to do our stunts on their own—they could *really* get hurt!

When I joined the Jesse White Tumblers, I was the youngest, so I became a kind of team mascot. Vernon named me "Baby Smurf." We call Vernon "Dohickey"; everyone has a nickname.

I didn't like being the youngest because everyone used to pick on me, but I mess around with the younger kids now. Being on the team is like being in a big family with lots of brothers and sisters.

That's little Gene racing with a boy who challenged him before a show. Gene is seven years old. Right now, he's the youngest tumbler, and he's good. Vernon is teaching Gene.

I'm in shows with the Jesse White Tumbling Team most of the year. Sometimes we perform at professional football or basketball games and sometimes for an art fair or a block party. We go to a lot of schools, too. If we're going to a faraway city like Miami, Florida, we'll fly. On shorter trips we might use a chartered bus, but usually we travel in the two vans. Sometimes the team splits up so we can go to more places.

If the show starts at one o'clock, you have to be at the office at twelve. If you lose your uniform, you can't perform, and you have to buy another one.

Germaine is next to Mr. White in the van. (That's Germaine on the cover of this book, too. He's the one zooming over everyone else.) He's sixteen, and he's the best tumbler. He can do a

"Punch-front." That's a series of five or six fast back flip-flops, then a forward flip. I can almost do that combination, but I can't quite get my balance afterwards.

While he drives the van, Mr. White talks to us about the show, about school, about being ladies and gentlemen, about everything. I like the way he talks, and I like the way he dresses when he's not wearing his team uniform. He's got style. Mr. White taught school for thirty years. He's an Illinois State Representative, and he works for the Chicago Board of Education. He's been a lot of different things including a paratrooper and a professional baseball player. He started the tumbling team in 1959. When he was growing up, he lived for a while in my neighborhood.

Before the show, Mr. White talks to the crowd. He says that most of us are from fatherless homes. Many kids in projects get in trouble with the law at some point, but hardly any of the tumblers have been in trouble because of the rules about staying in school and staying away from drinking, drugs, gangs, or any kind of crime.

One of the tumblers graduated from the University of Notre Dame School of Law. Others have become electricians, carpenters, policemen, teachers, and postal workers, or are in the military. One is a fashion designer. Almost nine hundred kids have been on the team.

Mr. White says his program is designed to teach young people that there's a lot more within them than they think. He says, "A quitter never wins, and a winner never quits."

When the show is about to begin, we bring out the mats and set up the speakers for our music. The music booms out, loud and rhythmic, and the crowd gets excited. We start doing warmup exercises—rolls, dives, and somersaults.

Then we do the "Floorwalk." Not everybody can do it. You don't have to put your hands down any special way, but your body has to be straight, and you have to keep your legs together.

SHOE
REPAIR

Enjoy
Coca-Cola

McDonald's

Enjoy Coca-Cola

PORTER

3 2359 00125 5829

After the Floorwalk, we do all kinds of tumbling stunts. Here's Vernon doing the "Dive" at a neighborhood block party. He runs to the mat, then leaps off the ground over his teammates. He can jump that high because when he hits the tip of the mat, he uses all his leg power. Mr. White sometimes likes to kid the audience. He says we can fly through the air because we have springs in our legs. And he always says we have a special way of getting high—without alcohol or drugs.

This trick is called the "Low Bridge." You have to run and then do a somersault in the air over the bridge of the other tumblers. Before you land, you uncurl yourself—that's what I'm doing in the picture—so you can land on your feet and "walk out."

Here is Mr. White holding me upside down while Omar is going over us. Omar is doing a trick called the ''V.'' Sometimes when it's hot and I'm upside down a lot, I get headaches.

Now Sam is supporting me while the team does the V at the Lincoln Avenue Street Fair. All the people crowd around because they want to see the show. They get in the way, but we're careful never to crash into them.

The first trick I learned was a "Flip-flop Back," which is a backwards flip. You need to learn this from someone who is a real expert. Your teacher holds your back while you do a backbend. When your hands touch the ground, you whip your legs over. You practice over and over, making your legs rotate faster. When your teacher thinks you've got it, you try to flip without him holding you. Doing a Flip-flop Back without hands is harder—it took me about a year to learn that.

If you do several moves together, for instance a Flip-flop Back, then a Somersault Back, then two Flip-flops Back, it's called a "combination" or a "set." We do lots of combinations in each show.

On some weekends we do 7 shows in a day. I'm really tired after 7 shows; I feel like I don't have legs anymore, and I can barely walk. I just want to go to sleep. But I perform because I have to. Mr. White says we must tell ourselves, "I'm dead tired, but I'm alive and well and kicking, and the show must go on." Last year we did 570 shows and went to twenty different states.

This stunt is called a "Baroni"—it's a front somersault with a half twist. You jump off a little trampoline called a "trampolette" or "mini-tramp." When I'm upside down, I don't have a chance to see how the world looks. Everything happens too fast.

Here I am doing the "High Bridge." It's much harder to do than the Low Bridge because you have to jump so high. You have to run fast, put all your weight onto the tramp, and then—make sure you don't hit anybody! In this picture I'm still gliding. Next I'm going to tuck my legs in and duck my head, completing a somersault before I land. After I land, I'll do a forward roll.

This year we performed at 65 professional sporting events: baseball, football, soccer, and basketball. Here we are at a Chicago Bears' game. Behind me are Chet and Germaine—we're watching the Bears make a point after a touchdown. In this picture I think I look like Gene!

At halftime, we go onto Soldier Field. It's really wet and cold, and my feet are freezing. I feel like I can hardly move, and Mr. White is yelling for us to pick up speed! Monica is in front, then Penelope—her mom works in Mr. White's office—then me.

We're doing the Floorwalk at Soldier Field. There are about sixty thousand fans here today.

When I'm out in front of everyone, I feel good inside. I like to think everyone is looking at me.

Kendra is doing some good Flip-flops.

We call this "Going over Mr. White." That's Tydell in the air.

Here's the team warming up before a Chicago Bulls' basketball game. In the picture below, Ronnie is doing the High Bridge. Basketball games are my favorites, and my favorite teams are the Chicago Bulls and the Los Angeles Lakers.

We do shows all over town. This one is at the opening of a new restaurant near the Robert Taylor housing project in Chicago. That's Bruce going over the "Pyramid." He looks like Superman. Some kids even call him Superman, but I like to call him Bruce.

David is going over the "Curtain." We're at an art fair.

That's me doing the "Human Chain." It's our most outstanding stunt, and we always do it last in the show. Bruce can go over twenty of us all lined up. I can go over fourteen people, which is a lot for someone my size. I'm only four feet ten inches right now, but I hope I'll be growing a lot this year.

When the audience sees us setting up to do this stunt, they think it's impossible, and each time we add more kids to the line they get more scared. I can see them grabbing their hearts. When a tumbler makes it over, they go *Aahhh,* and then they cheer.

Here I am "flying" again, this time in the other direction. To me, doing the Human Chain doesn't *really* feel like flying. It feels sort of like I'm lying down, asleep. I see the backs of the other tumblers, and I just hope I'm going to make it all the way over. I do a somersault in the middle of the trick. When I see the last person, then I know I've made it. It's a long way to go, and sometimes I'm scared I'll hit someone. When I'm in the chain, I just hope the person flying over doesn't land on me!

You know when you're not going to make it. When you wipe out, on the Human Chain or any of the stunts, you must go back and do the trick over again, right away.

The other tumblers are congratulating me because I made it, and they liked my fly.

The show takes about twenty minutes. At the end we do a backward somersault, and then we bow. We pick up the mats and leave.

We receive money for our shows. I buy food and clothes with some of my money, and I give some to my grandmother.

Because I'm a Jesse White Tumbler, I get to see a lot of places. I like traveling. I used to think everyplace was like Cabrini-Green. A few years ago Mr. White took me and another tumbler to Tokyo to appear on a Japanese television show honoring the twelve best youth teams in the world, kids with terrific sports skills. There were Japanese tumblers and Chinese acrobats and an English girl who was a weightlifter, and the judges said we were the best!

As soon as we got to Japan they wanted us to eat sushi—that's raw fish. After that, we found some hamburgers! We stayed in a really nice hotel. There were clocks in the lobby showing what time it was all over the world. It was fourteen hours earlier in Chicago.

Tokyo surprised me—it was nice and clean, with small streets and very tall buildings. Another place that surprised me was Iowa —it was so hot and dry. I was even surprised the first time I went to a suburb of Chicago because it was so clean and the buildings were different from Cabrini-Green—people had houses with lawns instead of apartments.

The Jesse White Tumblers have been on "Good Morning America," "The David Letterman Show," "USA Today," and in a commercial. And now we're going to be in a feature-length movie.

When I'm not working in a show, I like to mess around with
the other tumblers. That's Vernon spraying water on me. He's good
with the younger kids. I'm getting pretty wet, but I'm having fun.

I don't know what I want to be when I grow up. Maybe an actor—a star. I almost feel like I'm a star now because other kids look up to me. I hope to go to college. Maybe I'll get an athletic scholarship.

I would like to get married someday, but I don't want kids. I have too many little cousins!

I wouldn't say I've had a hard life. I've had an easy life—very easy, because I haven't gotten into trouble. Being on the team has helped me a lot.

That's me, freezing. I go to a park near my house where I practice by myself two days a week. I go even if it's cold.

Being in the Jesse White Tumblers makes me happy. If for some reason I couldn't be on the team, I'd be very hurt. I'd miss the tumbling and the trips and my friends. And I think my friends would miss me.

See you at the show!

Diane Schmidt is a photojournalist living in Chicago. Her books include *The Chicago Exhibition, Abstract Relations,* and *Where's Chimpy?* a book for children. Her work has also been published, both nationally and internationally, in many books and magazines. She has been interviewed on national TV and radio programs and is the recipient of an Arts Midwest/National Endowment for the Arts grant. Recently she has especially enjoyed taking pictures of Kenyon and his teammates for this book.

Diane has a niece named Sarah who is six and a dog named Emily who is ten. The three of them like to go for long walks together along Lake Michigan.

photo by Sally Good